SALISBURY CATHEDRAL

by the late Canon A. F. Smethurst, Ph.D., M.A., B.Sc.

THE Cathedral Church of the Blessed Virgin Mary at Salisbury is famous rather for its beauty and artistic merit than for its historical associations. It cannot compare with some other English cathedrals, such as Winchester or St. Paul's, in historical significance, nor is it rich in tombs of kings or national heroes—though King Henry III was present at its consecration and many other royalty have worshipped here. But it is a splendid and graceful work of architecture, in the loveliest setting of any cathedral in this country; and its superb spire is renowned throughout the world, thanks in part to the paintings of John Constable. It symbolises the peaceful loveliness of the English countryside amidst which it stands, the eternal truths of the Christian Faith expressed in stone, and the continuing worship of Almighty God.

For more than 3,500 years Wiltshire and the district around Salisbury has been a centre of religious worship. At Stonehenge, ten miles north of the city, a temple has stood since about 1800 B.C.; and this, with its later great Stone Circle, is probably the best known of all British archaeological remains. At Avebury, some 35 miles north of Salisbury, is a slightly earlier and much larger ancient sanctuary. Thus in the dawn of our history primitive men worshipped their gods in this area and we can still visit the impressive remains of their temples and burial places.

With the Romans the Christian religion was first brought to England; and at Old Sarum, on the summit of

a chalk hill about two miles north of the present cathedral of Salisbury, they found an Early Iron Age fortified town, enclosed by a large earth wall. This they used as a fortress; and by A.D. 160 it was called Sorbiodunum. They made it an important centre of communications, a meeting-place of many great Roman roads. Later the Saxons increased its fortifications, and it became a notable town under the name of Seares byrig. Finally William

the Conqueror reviewed and disbanded his army there in 1070, and the Normans reconstructed the defences and built a royal military castle, the ruins of which can still be seen.

Many of the Saxon cathedrals had been in small villages; but in 1075 it was enacted that the sees of all bishops should be removed to cities or larger towns. Accordingly the two dioceses of Sherborne and Ramsbury, then both held by Bishop Herman,

Continued on page 6

★

FACING PAGE: *The nave, looking east. This view shows the purity and austerity of the design, which reflects the influence of the Cistercian buildings of the same period.*

RIGHT: *One of the four Bending columns upon which rest the tower and the spire. The columns were not originally designed to support a weight in excess of an estimated 6,400 tons. As a consequence, they are slightly bent.*

3

SALISBURY CATHEDRAL

CONSECRATED 1258

ABOVE: *The cathedral from across the River Avon, a view made famous by the painter Constable.*

FACING PAGE: *The north transept, in which are the chapel of St. Thomas of Canterbury and the chapel of St. Edmund Rich.*

ABOVE: *The great west window was composed in its present form in 1824 and contains some of the finest glass in the cathedral. The seven shields were taken from the Chapter House and with one exception date from 1270–1280. The figure panels are of the 15th and 16th centuries and were brought from France.*

MEMORIAE
RICARDI·COLT·HOARE·BARONETTI
DOMO·STOVRHEAD·IN·COM·WILTON

were formally united into one new diocese, and its see was fixed at Old Sarum, because that was both a centre of communications and a city with a royal castle.

Old Sarum consists of an irregular oval of ground nearly a mile in circumference, enclosed by a wide and deep ditch. In the middle of this is a smaller and nearly circular earthwork, within which are the remains of the Norman castle. About a quarter of the space inside the outer ditch or wall was given to the bishop for his cathedral and the houses of his clergy; and here Herman began to build the first cathedral of the new diocese. But in 1078 he died, and it was his successor, St. Osmund, who completed it. It was finished in 1092. Only five days after its consecration it was very severely damaged by lightning; and in the early part of the next century it was rebuilt. Very little remains of either the small Norman cathedral of St. Osmund, or the larger Norman building of his successor, Bishop Roger, with crypt, transepts and cloisters; but the foundations have been traced out, and can be very clearly seen. For this reason, as well as on account of the ruins of the castle, Old Sarum is well worth a visit. The total length of St. Osmund's church was 173 feet, that of Bishop Roger's 316 feet, while that of the exterior of the present cathedral is considerably greater, being 473 feet.

St. Osmund was a Norman who accompanied William the Conqueror when he came to England in 1066. He was Chancellor of England from 1074 to 1078, being, like most of the ablest and most learned men of that time, a priest. On the death of Herman he was consecrated bishop of Sarum. He died in 1099. His greatest work was not in the actual building of the cathedral, but in the planning of its worship and activities. Salisbury Cathedral has never at any time, either at Old Sarum or at its present site, been administered or controlled by monks. Osmund, with all his wisdom and experience of administration as Chancellor of the Realm, laid down the constitution and statutes of his cathedral, regulating the way in which it was to be managed and maintained. So well did he do it that the arrangements at Salisbury became the model for many other cathedrals, not only in England but also in Scotland and even in France, though he owed something to earlier French and Norman models.

Osmund decreed that the cathedral was to be ruled by a Chapter or Brotherhood of Canons, led by four *Personae* or Principal Persons—the Dean, who presided; the Precentor, responsible for the choir and music; the Chancellor, who was Secretary of the Chapter and had the oversight of all the schools and colleges in the city, the education of the clergy and the library; and the Treasurer, who had charge of all the ornaments, vestments and other costly treasures of the cathedral. There were subordinate clergy concerned with the singing and other activities.

The duties of the *personae* and canons were clearly defined by St. Osmund, and the cathedral is still controlled mainly by his constitution. In addition he was keenly interested in the music and choir, and founded the Song School, which has continued to this day, being now a flourishing preparatory school of a hundred and thirty boys, which provides for the education and boarding of the sixteen boy choristers of the cathedral. He probably also initiated a tradition of reverent and dignified ceremonial in the services, which was developed at Salisbury by Bishop Richard Poore when the present cathedral was built,

*

ABOVE: *The memorial in the north transept to Richard Colt Hoare, the Wiltshire historian, whose study can still be seen in Stourhead House.*

FACING PAGE: *The works of the oldest clock in England. Made c. 1386, the clock was originally installed in the detached bell tower which was demolished in 1790. From then until 1884 the clock was in the central tower of the cathedral.*

so that the services there became so splendid and so well carried out that they were famous all over England, and served as a model for many churches throughout the land. Finally in 1542, at the time of the Reformation, it was directed that until a Prayer Book in English had been drawn up, all churches in the Province must follow "The Use of Sarum," as the forms of service and ceremonies used at Salisbury were called.

Both the Roman and the Saxon names for Old Sarum mean "dry fortress" or "dry city"; and it was indeed dry and very short of water, being on the summit of a hill with chalky subsoil. The cathedral was within the "line of fire" from the castle; the wind was terrible "so that the clerks can hardly hear one another sing" and they suffered from severe rheumatism, and the church was continually damaged; there were not sufficient houses for the clergy within the congested city; and finally the soldiers in the castle were frequently annoying them and interfering with the services. So in 1217 Richard Poore, who had in that year been made bishop after having been dean of the cathedral for 19 years, petitioned the Pope for leave to remove his cathedral elsewhere. This was granted; and with the king's support he began in 1220 to build a new cathedral on land which was his own property, having been refused ground at Wilton by the abbess there. The site he chose was unlikely to suffer from a shortage of water, for it lies at a point where two other rivers flow into the Avon.

The building of the new cathedral was placed under the supervision of one of the canons, Elias de Dereham, who is associated with other famous buildings, such as the great hall of Winchester Castle. To what extent he actually designed the building in detail is uncertain. He was assisted by a famous master mason, Nicholas of Ely. The first section to be built was the Chapel of the Holy Trinity and All Saints at the east end (wrongly known as the "Lady Chapel"—the whole cathedral is dedicated to Our Lady, the Blessed Virgin Mary). This was completed and dedicated in 1225, and in the following year the bodies of three of the bishops of Old Sarum, including that of St. Osmund, were brought down and re-interred in the new cathedral. Over St. Osmund's body was later erected a rich stone shrine, probably ornamented with

gold, and later furnished with a very costly reliquary to contain his skull.

To this pilgrims came in great numbers after St. Osmund had been canonized in 1457. In 1790 the remains of the shrine were removed to the south side of the nave, where it still stands; but a plain slab of black Purbeck stone, now on the south-west side of the Trinity Chapel, marked his grave, and to this a solemn procession of clergy and people still goes every year at evensong on the anniversary of his death—4th December. The tombs of Bishop Roger and another bishop from Old Sarum are now at the extreme south-west end of the nave.

In 1228 Bishop Poore was made Bishop of Durham; but the whole interior of the cathedral was finished to the original design, and Salisbury is thus the only English cathedral, except St. Paul's, of which the whole interior structure was built to the design of one man and completed without a break. All this, except the

west front, was carried out by Nicholas of Ely; that, with the cloisters and Chapter House, was the work of Richard the Mason.

The Trinity Chapel is the most daring and original part of the whole building. Its roof rises from two rows of very slender pillars of black Purbeck marble, and between these and the side walls are two very narrow side-aisles, above which the roof consists of a series of sharply pointed arches. At the west end of the chapel are two further Purbeck pillars, each enclosed by four extremely thin pillars of the same stone. The effect is very remarkable.

The departure of Bishop Richard Poore broke up a Chapter of very great distinction. Included in it in his day was another very saintly and learned man, St. Edmund (Rich) of Abingdon, treasurer of the cathedral and afterwards Archbishop of Canterbury. His holy character, Bishop Poore's learning, ability and goodness, and the reputation of others of the

canons for scholarship, resulted in many students coming hither from Oxford, and several colleges were founded in Salisbury in that century. Notable among them were the College of St. Edmund (named after Edmund Rich) dating from 1269, with the fine church of St. Edmund attached to it (now redundant, this is used as an arts centre); and the College of St. Nicholas de Vaux, founded in 1261, which formerly stood just outside the south (Harnham) gate of the Close. With these and other colleges for clergy and students, Salisbury almost became a university at that time. The Close still to this day remains a centre of education, having in it a theological college for ordinands, the Cathedral School, a boys' grammar school (Bishop Wordsworth's), and two private schools, while the Godolphin School, a public school for girls, was started in the Close and is still in the city.

Before 1227 there also existed another foundation dedicated to St. Nicholas, from which the College de Vaux obtained its name. This is the Hospital of St. Nicholas, "for receiving and supporting the poor." It still retains some of its medieval buildings, and still serves the same purpose as an almshouse for aged men and women. It has a warden and chaplain; and it is said to be the original of "Hiram's Hospital" in Trollope's novel *The Warden*. The hospital is situated just across the road to the old Harnham Bridge, which was built by Bishop Bingham in 1245 and had on it a small chapel dedicated to St. John, which still exists though it ceased to be a chapel in the 16th century.

In addition to "designing" the cathedral, Elias de Dereham is said to have made the first new tomb to be erected in the cathedral. This is the effigy of William Longespée, the elder, a son of King Henry II, half-brother to King John. He was Earl of Salisbury, and in 1220 laid one of the foundation stones of the cathedral. Longespée's wife, the saintly Ela, founded Lacock Abbey; and his son, also commemorated in the cathedral by an effigy in the north aisle, was a famous warrior and general of the English crusaders, who died in battle at Mansoura.

The work of building went on fast; and at the same time houses were built around the cathedral for the canons and other clergy, and also for the workmen and others. Several of the oldest houses still remaining in the

★

ABOVE: *The Sanctuary. It was altered in 1960 when a large Victorian reredos was removed, and has three eastern arches with rich, deep mouldings.*

FACING PAGE: *The Chantry of Bishop Edward Audley (died 1524), with its fine fan tracery, is the only chantry chapel remaining in order and in use. The Virgin and Child above the altar was painted in Florence.*

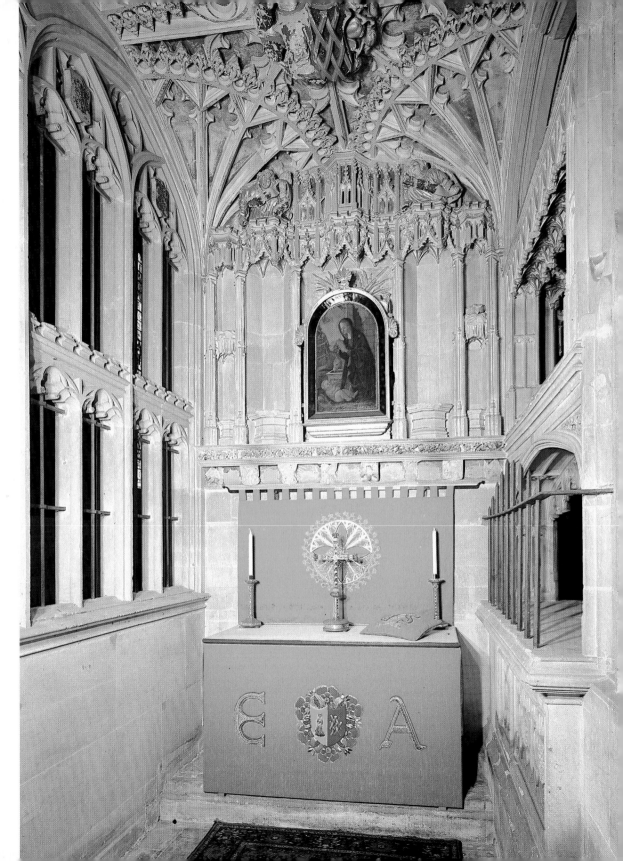

Close were first built at this time; while the earliest streets of the city were constructed to the north and east of the Close, crossing at right angles to form squares called "Chequers." Many of these still exist, with small medieval houses in them. From these soon grew the city of "New Sarum" or Salisbury.

By 1258 the choir, transepts and nave were completed, except for the west front; and on 30th September it was consecrated, Giles de Bridport being bishop. The west front was added almost at once, and by 1265 all was finished. Meanwhile it had been decided to build cloisters; and these, dating from about 1263–1270, are the earliest ones in any English cathedral. They suffered sadly from misuse and neglect in the 17th and 18th centuries, and at present are greatly in need of cleaning, repair and redecoration; but they are noble specimens of Geometrical Decorated architecture, and enclose a lovely quiet Cloister Garth, in which are now buried the ashes of bishops and *personae.*

One purpose of the cloisters was to provide a passage from the cathedral to the Chapter House, which was constructed about 1263–1284, also by Richard the Mason. This is the chamber in which the business of the Chapter was conducted. It is a superb example of Geometrical Decorated style, similar to that of Westminster Abbey. It rises from a single central pillar from which the roof fans out, and it is octagonal in shape. Round the sides runs a stone plinth with seats for the canons, and at the east end are raised seats for the bishop, dean and dignitaries. Above the niches of the seats and below the windows runs a series of 60 stone bas-reliefs, also dating from the end of the 13th century though well restored in the 19th. They depict Old Testament stories, including the Six Days of Creation, Adam and Eve, Noah and the Flood, Abraham and the Patriarchs, Joseph, Moses, and the Giving of the Ten Commandments. They are most vivid and admirable examples of medieval sculpture. Between each niche is a carved face of contemporary date. At the bottom of the spring of each arch of the nave roof is a similar sculptured face; and all these examples of 13th-century sculpture (as well as those over the outside of the entrance to the Chapter House which represent fourteen virtues triumphing over vices) well repay study, though usually pass quite unnoticed.

The Chapter House was badly damaged in Cromwell's time, and had to be extensively repaired and restored in the middle of last century. The glass in the windows was so badly broken that it had to be removed, the best fragments of it being embodied in the present Great West Window,
Continued on page 15

*

ABOVE: *A portion of the ancient choir screen which dates from c. 1260. It originally divided the choir from the nave and was removed to the Morning Chapel in 1790.*

FACING PAGE: *One of the Strainer arches at the entrance to the choir transept. They differ in design from those in the main transepts and were erected late in the 14th century to prevent the great piers collapsing inwards.*

ABOVE: *The Trinity Chapel. The window contains the new glass by Gabriel Loire to commemorate Prisoners* *of Conscience of the 20th century, giving a blaze of colour in the east.* FACING PAGE: *A view of the entire* *length of the cathedral from the Trinity Chapel, looking west. The length of the nave is about 230 feet.*

including six heraldic shields. New glass of a dull pattern was inserted instead; but the restoration of the Chapter House itself was well done.

When the whole of the interior of the cathedral and its outbuildings was completed, it represented a splendid achievemant of architecture in the English Gothic style.

It was built of oolitic Jurassic Portland limestone from the quarries at Chilmark, ten miles west of Salisbury—a fine white stone, which

★

FACING PAGE: *The tomb of Sir Thomas Gorges and his wife, Helena Snachenberg of Sweden. He was a courtier and she was a maid of honour to Queen Elizabeth I. The window, by Christopher Webb, commemorates the poet George Herbert (1593–1633).*

ABOVE: *The St. Osmond Ledger Stone (in foreground) once marked the position of the grave of St. Osmond, who completed the cathedral at Old Sarum. The slab was removed to its present position after the Reformation.*

weathers light grey. The pillars are of dark "marble" brought from a quarry at Worth Matravers in the Isle of Purbeck. The great merits of the building are its clarity, unity, and simplicity. Its design is that of a great cross with two arms, and nothing disturbs this plan. Its series of windows in the top storey or clerestory illuminates the simple but delicate roof, and the clerestory and triforium together give great height and spaciousness to the nave. Though not the largest of English cathedrals, Salisbury is among the bigger, the total length of the interior being 449 feet, the breadth of the nave and aisles 78 feet, the height of the nave 85 feet, and its length about 230 feet. The interior is often said to look cold, on account of lack of colour. This is partly because the stone has only a faint delicate tint and there is little old stained glass left; but when it was built the walls were decorated with black scroll work on a red ground, the capitals of the shafts and other mouldings were gilt and coloured, and the vaults of the roof were mainly white, so that the effect must have been striking and lovely.

But the most perfect part of the

whole cathedral was added a hundred years after the main building—namely, the spire. This famous landmark was built between 1285 and 1310. It was the work of an unknown master mason and it was a truly stupendous achievement. The earlier builders had left the tower very squat, rising only a few feet above the level of the nave roof; and the piers and foundations below this very small tower were not constructed to carry much more weight than elsewhere in the building. Moreover a passage was cut through them in the triforium and clerestory. In spite of this the master mason boldly placed on them two further stages of the tower—distinguishable clearly from the lowest level by their long windows and rich decoration—and above this constructed a great spire rising to a height of 404 feet. It was built around interior wood scaffolding, which was left there when it was completed and still remains, together with the old wooden windlass which was used to raise the materials to the bottom of the spire—and is still so used.

The immense load on the four main piers, six feet square, of more than 6,400 tons, puts a tremendous strain

Continued on page 19

ABOVE: *The tomb of Giles de Bridport who was bishop when the cathedral was consecrated in 1258 and who died in 1262. The carvings represent scenes from his life.*
FACING PAGE: *A view of the nave from the south choir aisle seen through one of the stone girder-arches added by Bishop Beauchamp in the 15th century.*

on them. To meet this the builders made a strong stone vault at the crossing of the nave below the tower, and this is an excellent specimen of the Decorated style, in contrast to the Early English of the rest of the interior. They also built into the thickness of the clerestory walls an extensive system of internal stone buttresses to resist the thrust of the main arches on all four sides, and a group of external flying-buttresses rising off the main aisle walls up to the tower.

In spite of all these precautions the great stress on the supporting walls caused the pillars to bend and the walls to shift slightly; and in the 15th century Bishop Beauchamp had two great stone girder-arches added at the entrances to the main transepts between the piers supporting the spire. These arches are incidentally fine examples of the Perpendicular style, and are ornamented with excellent—and sometimes humorous —carved heads. Earlier, double arches (the inverted arches above the main ones) were added in the choir transepts.

All these precautions succeeded in counteracting the stresses, and the tower and spire settled with a displacement of only three and a half inches. But the bending of the piers under the strain imposed on them can be very clearly seen by looking upwards from the bottom of them. The spire has a declination of $29\frac{1}{2}$ inches to the south-west. This was determined in 1668 by Sir Christopher Wren when he surveyed the cathedral, and again in 1737, when a small brass plate was inserted in the floor of the nave to mark the spot touched by a plumbline suspended from near the top of the spire. No movement was found, nor in 1951 when the determination was repeated. So it is clear that the spire is safe from further movement under normal conditions. It has, however, given anxiety in other ways. The original builders, Wren in the 17th century, and Sir Gilbert Scott in the

★

19th, all strengthened the spire with iron supports and ties and bands. But in 1950 it was found that these had rusted, and as a result of this and of the weather the stone of the uppermost thirty feet had become so decayed that it was necessary to rebuild this section of the spire completely. However, erosion by the weather and atmospheric pollution during the past 25 years has caused serious weakening of spire and tower, and repairs at an estimated cost of £6,500,000, taking ten

years to complete, are in progress. So the great spire, the highest in England, and second highest in Europe, and by common consent the most lovely of all, is being preserved. Its grace, delicacy and height, added to the natural "feminine" charm and lightness of the exterior of the building, rising out of its great green lawn and set among the lovely houses of the Close, creates the unique beauty of Salisbury Cathedral.

In 1445 the bishop and chapter built a library over the eastern cloister,

reached by a winding stone stairway from the south-west corner of the south transept. This building was originally twice its present length, and included the Chancellor's Lecture Room. It contains many very ancient manuscripts, 187 in all, of which two of the finest are a Gallican Psalter of the 10th century, in Latin, with an interlinear gloss in Anglo-Saxon, and another Gallican Psalter of the 10th century, containing names of old Breton Saints. The earliest manuscript of all is a page of the Old Testament in Latin dating from the 8th century.

Among other treasures are *Fons Jacobi*, a 15th-century devotional book in English of which no other copy exists, and several old service books, such as a unique Tonale of the 14th century, beautifully illuminated and with the music shown in full; a Processionale of the 15th century; and a glorious large illuminated Breviary of the 15th century. Many of the other MSS are of the 9th–13th centuries. Salisbury also possesses over 30 early printed books dating from before

1500, including Caxton's *Golden Legend* printed by his partner, Wynken de Worde. Another unique section of the library consists of a remarkable collection of early scientific, mathematical and medical books bequeathed by Bishop Seth Ward, who before becoming Bishop of Salisbury in 1667 had been Professor of Astronomy at Oxford and a founder member of the Royal Society. Among these is William Harvey's *De Motu Cordis*, in which the circulation of the blood was first announced.

But most famous of all is the copy of Magna Carta. This is one of the four contemporary copies of the document in existence, and is more perfect than any of the others, though lacking the seal. The document is now on display to the public in the Chapter House.

Salisbury Cathedral has from time to time needed extensive repair and restoration, especially in the interior. After the deplorable attacks of ignorant iconoclasts, at the Reformation and during the Commonwealth, it was in a shocking state when Seth Ward

became bishop, and that great man asked his friend Sir Christopher Wren to survey it. Wren's manuscript notes on its condition, and suggested remedies, are preserved in the library, and in his time the choir was repaired and refurnished. But during the middle of the 18th century it was again allowed to fall into a bad state of repair; and finally in 1789–92 James Wyatt, architect of Fonthill Abbey and Wilton House cloisters, was called in to restore it.

★

ABOVE: *The chapel of Margaret of Scotland (1045–1093), wife of Malcolm III of Scotland and granddaughter of the English king Edmund Ironside. Now used as the Mothers' Union Chapel.*

FACING PAGE, top: *A view of the cloisters across the cloister garth. They were built about 1263–1270.*

FACING PAGE, bottom: *The interior of the cloisters, which are the oldest in any English cathedral. They are in the Geometrical Decorated style.*

Wyatt has been violently criticised, mostly for what he took away. First, the detached bell-tower, like that of Chichester. (You can still in dry weather see the outline of its foundations to the left of the path as you start for the north porch.) Its wooden upper stage had gone, the bells had been given away, and it was thought to block the view of the cathedral; the Dean and Chapter had little money, and the architect was dependent on the energetic bishop and the purposes for which he wanted his money spent.

Secondly, two 15th-century chantry chapels, in memory of Bishop Beauchamp and Lord Robert Hungerford, had been built into the walls either side of the Trinity Chapel. One had curious paintings. They were in bad repair; they no longer served a purpose; and Wyatt shared the (probably mistaken) view that their building had dangerously weakened the Chapel's delicate walls. We regret their loss when we see old prints of the cathedral and compare the beauty of the surviving Audley chantry.

Thirdly, he abolished the high altar, treating the eastern part of the church from the choir screen eastward as one church, with the Trinity Chapel as the chancel. (It didn't work; the high altar was back in thirty years.) He used stone and ornament from the demolished chantry chapels to make a reredos for the Trinity Chapel altar. Then he moved the remains of the 13th-century choir screen to the west wall of the "morning chapel" (where you still see the gilding on the stone angels' wings), and built a fine larger screen to carry the new great organ presented by George III as a gentleman of Berkshire (which was in the diocese till 1836), with more stone from the chantries. He made fine canopies for the choir stalls; Seth Ward's had been removed as "too gaudy" ten years earlier. He limewashed the high vaults throughout the church to hide the faded medieval colour.

Fourthly, he removed from the windows the remainder of the 13th-century stained glass, and replaced it with clear glazing. Fifthly, he removed the gravestones from the Close, which shocked his contemporaries, and inside the building he moved several tombs from the Trinity Chapel and arranged most of them tidily upon the plinth in the nave.

Now for the credit side. When he moved the gravestones, he also drained the standing water and gave us the open expanse of grass which is one of our glories. The removal of the bell-tower and the chantry chapels actually restored the original plan of the building; we still see quite unaltered the textbook Early English church, and see it clearly. Moving the tombs inside gave us the clear uncluttered space of the Trinity Chapel.

The new glass in the Five Lancets at the east end, dedicated to Prisoners of Conscience, offers a blaze of colour to catch the eye of the morning and the eye of the visitor and the inner eye of the worshipper; to counteract the predominant sense of greyness, and

★

ABOVE: *The beautiful fan vaulting of the Chapter House rising from the single central pillar.*

FACING PAGE: *The Chapter House, which is in the Geometrical Decorated style, c. 1280, was the original conference room of the Chapter. The building has now been converted into an exhibtion area displaying the original Magna Carta document, silver and other archives. Along the frieze above the niches is a series of 13th-century sculptures, depicting Old Testament stories.*

on nearer observation to speak to the heart of those who are prepared to stand and look and read what is written in the glass and hear what the window is saying.

A man that looks on glasse,
    On it may stay his eye;
Or if he pleaseth, through it passe,
    And then the heav'n espie.
        (George Herbert 1593–1633)

About 1870 the first Sir Gilbert Scott undid all Wyatt's work in the choir. George III's organ was given to St. Thomas's church, and Wyatt's fine screen was not needed; the pipes of the new Willis organ were to be either side of the choir. So Wyatt's screen was replaced by Skidmore's open metal screen. Scott supplied an alabaster reredos for the high altar, the present nave pulpit and a new Gothic floor. He removed Wyatt's choir stalls (the present canopies date from 1913), and reproduced the medieval paintings once more on the high vaults and on the Trinity Chapel vault. Like Wyatt, he too inspected and made safe the tower and spire.

His decoration has not on the whole commended itself to his successors. Between 1959 and 1963 the screen and reredos went, leaving the unbroken vista which many people value: and after that the Trinity Chapel and choir were repaved and refurnished. During the last 30 years the old side-chapels have been brought back into use, and several new stained glass windows have been put in.

There are three good modern windows: by Christopher Webb, the George Herbert window at the end of the north choir aisle, and the City war memorial window in the north nave aisle; by Stammers of York, the Glider Pilot Regiment window, by the north porch.

As has already been stated, the oldest houses in the Close were erected while the cathedral was not yet completed. Among these is the old Bishop's Palace, now the Cathedral School. The earliest part is Bishop Poore's undercroft of 1220, now the boys' dining-room. Above it Bishop Sherlock's fine drawing room of 1745, recently redecorated, had replaced Poore's Great Hall. The north porch and chapel are 15th-century; Seth Ward was responsible for the 17th-century staircase and the homely south front.

The Close itself was completely walled-in about 1333. In 1331 King

Edward III gave the bishop and chapter all the stones from the old cathedral and canons' houses at Old Sarum for the building of the Close wall: and the Norman carving may still be seen on these stones. The wall encloses the Close on two sides, and has four gates. The other two sides are enclosed by the river. Thus Salisbury Close is still a real Close, in addition to being the largest and most beautiful in England. Among its houses are "Hemyngsby", with a medieval hall and chapel; "Aula le Stage"; the King's House where King James I stayed; the North Canonry, with a magnificent medieval gateway; Mompesson House, built in 1701, now the property of the National Trust and a splendid example of the period; and the Walton Canonry, where the fisherman Izaak Walton lived with his son, a canon. There are many other superb examples of 17th- and 18th-century houses, including the Choir School and Wren Hall, and the Matrons' College erected by Seth Ward to house the widows of clergymen from his two dioceses of Exeter and Salisbury, much in the style of his friend Wren.

Thus the cathedral stands in the midst of a quiet, secluded and most lovely setting; and what it lacks in history or grandeur when compared with some other cathedrals it more than makes up for in grace, loveliness and peace. But the main value of a cathedral is neither its architectural beauty nor its historical associations, but its maintenance of the worship of God. Day by day praise and prayer are offered here to Him with glorious music and reverent ceremonial; and the Cathedral Church of the Blessed Virgin Mary at Salisbury stands as a living witness to the Christian Faith today.

*

ABOVE: *The cathedral seen from the north-east. The spire is over 400 feet high and is the highest in England and second highest in Europe.*

ACKNOWLEDGMENTS

All the photographs in this book were taken by Gerald Newbery, F.I.I.P., F.R.P.S., excepting: page 1 by Kenneth Scowen, F.I.I.P., F.R.P.S.; pages 2, 8, 12 and 13 by Sonia Halliday and Laura Lushington; page 20 by David Miller; back cover by Aerofilms Limited.

SBN 85372 217 X